George Stephens, Collection Fiske Icelandic

The Runic Hall in the Danish Old-Northern Museum

George Stephens, Collection Fiske Icelandic

The Runic Hall in the Danish Old-Northern Museum

ISBN/EAN: 9783337735449

Printed in Europe, USA, Canada, Australia, Japan

Cover: Foto ©ninafisch / pixelio.de

More available books at **www.hansebooks.com**

THE RUNIC HALL

IN

THE DANISH OLD-NORTHERN MUSEUM.

BY

PROF. GEORGE STEPHENS, F. S. A.

—

CHEAPINGHAVEN (KØBENHAVN).

MICHAELSEN AND TILLGE.

PRINTED BY THIELE.

1868.

FOREWORD.

—

I have been requested to draw up a *short* account of the interesting and remarkable Runic Monuments now brought together in the Runic Hall of the Danish Museum of Northern Antiquities. I have consented so much the more willingly, as about half these pieces were already engraved and their inscriptions translated (some wholly or in part for the first time) in my «Old-Northern Runic Monuments of Scandinavia and England». To that and to other works I refer for fuller accounts.

State-Councilor Worsaae happily formed this Runic Hall in March 1867, tho it was not open to the public till some weeks after. And it was high time that these old-laves should at last be taken care of and conveniently placed. Some of them — for want of room — were lying stored in out-of-the-way places in the Museum; others were in the graveyard of Trinity Church, exposed to the hurtful elements; the rest were in the Round Tower, where most of them could scarcely be seen and all were being more or less damaged every day. Such venerable remains are best kept where they are found, or as near thereto as possible. But those which cannot be locally protected, and those which have no responsible owner, are most properly sheltered in a great Museum. It is to be hoped that this example will be followed, and that London, Newcastle, Edinburgh, Lund, Bergen, Christiania, Upsala, Stockholm, will soon have their Runic Halls as well as Cheapinghaven. Beginnings have already been made; but much remains to be done. The time has come when extensive collections of *Casts also* must be added, both for the study of our men of science and because many of these precious objects should not remain only in one copy. These monuments are of the utmost value to us. They bear the oldest remains of our written tung, *many hundreds of years* beyond our fornest skinbooks. They open up pictures of the life and death and exploits of our forefathers which cannot be found elsewhere. And they offer a striking proof of *the oneness* of all the Northern folkships. For the runes belong to the Northmen and the Northmen only. Found but in Scandinavia and its oldest settlement - England, they were unknown, as far back as we can go, to the Saxons and the Germans.

The oldest runic pieces in the Northern lands are in an alphabet best called *Old-Northern*, as being used in all the North, Scandia and England. This futhore has about double the number of staves to that which gradually prevailed later, and which may be best named the Scandinavian staverow, as being in use chiefly in Scandinavia; for in England the runes rapidly died out and were replaced by Latin letters, a change which afterwards took place in Scandia itself. The chief difference between the Old-Northern and the Scandian alphabet (most of whose characters are in common) is this, that the latter by degrees cast away many of the older letters, introduced a couple

of new marks, and gave to one or two others a different value. This curious and gradual movement
we can only imperfectly trace for want of monuments. Generally speaking, the older alphabet may
be lookt upon as introduced by the Northmen when they settled in these lands; the later staverow
would seem to have become nearly fixt about the 9th century. Several runic pieces are overgang,
bear still lingering older staves mixt with the Scandinavian. These transition-laves are usually
very old.

Of the older or Old-Northern letters Denmark has many examples, tho only one Danish
runestone entirely in the ancient runes is now known, the block from Voldtofte, Fyn, at present
deposited in the gardens of Jaegerspris. But several overgang stones remain.

It is in vain to deny that Denmark, as well as all the other Northern lands, has had
earthfast pieces bearing the older letters. For:

1. When these were *the only* runes used on all other the oldest objects, they would be
employed on stones also.

2. The many transition monuments point back to a time when the older letters alone
were in vogue; just as monuments with mixt Runic and Latin point to an age when only runic
characters were known.

3. Bleking was once probably a Danish folkland. But in Bleking are still several stones
with only the Old-Northern runes.

4. We *here* one such stone still left, that from Voldtofte.

5. Of course the *oldest* blocks are *first* to perish, and in comparatively stoneless Denmark
the destruction of these pieces has been immense. Therefore we cannot expect many to remain.
And even now such stones are often destroyed as soon as found.

Now it stands to reason that if *all* or *nearly all* the runic stones found in Denmark are
barbarously smasht as fast as they are found, we shall never be able to point out *Danish stones
with Old-Northern runes*. Finn Magnussen bitterly complained that in his time dozens of runic blocks
had been broken in pieces without even being copied, and several other such old-laves have in like
manner since been ruined. I have lately heard of a fresh example. A Danish gentleman tells me
that in May 1867 he visited Jutland. When at Skive he heard that a runic monument had been found
a few days before. He drove to the place, Haderup, about 3 Danish miles south of Skive, and talkt
with the finder. But he had come too late. The stone was beaten into many pieces, and all the
fragments had been used or thrown away. Counting the number of these blocks *destroyed in this
century* in Denmark at only 50, at least 5 or 4 or 3 *may* have been «Old-Northern».

In describing the handful of carved pieces brought together in the Runic Hall, it will be
convenient and instructive to take them in their chronological order, first the oldest then the younger.
But we have seldom any absolute certainty as to their exact date. The age of such objects can be
fixt only approximatively, due weight being given to the kind of letters, the antiquity of the language,
the style of the formula, and so on. I therefore beg pardon should I here and there have erred in
this particular.

VORDINGBORG, SEALAND.

VORDINGBORG, SEALAND.

† DATE ABOUT A. D. 600—700.

(See Prof. Nyerup. «Det af Kong Valdemar opbygte Vordingborg Slots ærværdige Ruiner» (Antiqvariske Annaler, Kjøbenhavn 1812, 8vo. Vol. 1, Page 41; Wormii Monumenta Danica, Fol., Page 128; G. Stephens «Old-Northern Runic Monuments», Fol., Page 335—7.)

This venerable granite minne-stone has suffered terribly, and is here and there only barely legible. It was first deciphered (rightly or wrongly is another question) by me in my O. N. R. Monuments. Doubtless it came from one of the heathen hows (tumuli) formerly found near Vordingborg, but it was first observed by the famous Chancelor Christian Fris of Kragerup in the middle of the 17th century, who saw it as a footstone under the Excise-Office in Vording-borg. At the proposal of the great Olaf Worm and by command of the King, Frederick III, it was transported to the capital (Trinity Churchyard). This was one of the 3 blocks which escaped the fire, and the barbarisms of Søren Mathiesen the Sexton. Afterwards it was deposited in the Round Tower, where it remained till the Runic Hall was formed in the Old-Northern Museum. Unhappily, at its removal thither in March 1867, it was broken in many pieces. It has since been carefully put together, and the damage is less than might have been expected. But I had made my drawings and engraving while it still stood in the Round Tower, and had also taken a Plaster Mould of the 1st runic line. This Mould I have given to the Museum for the consultation of students, and we can therefore «read the runes» as well as we could before.

During my labors I found the Old-Northern bind-rune ᚺᚹ low down on the stone, and identified the O. N. letters ᚤ (A) and ᛒ (C) in the body of the inscription. There is no more reason to call the above bind-rune «modern» than any other of the staves. It could not have been «forged» while the stone stood on its low (grave-mound), for that part of the block must then have been hidden in the earth. And to suppose it carved while the stone was «a footstone in the Excise-Office of Vordingborg» is a wild and ungrounded speculation. No «ignorant peasant» would or could at that time have forged what to him must have been a *Roman Monogram*. — In the same manner, low down on the Bårse stone, which see, we have the bind-rune ᚹ.

This block is 4-sided, total height about 4 feet 5 inches, total breadth (both the runic sides) about 3 feet 1 inch. The staves are from 3½ to 4 inches high, the bind-rune only 2½ inches. Still lower down are faint scorings which look like a reverst ᚾ (U I).

The ᚺᚹ (H W) may have signified any name beginning with H (for instance HAIRWULFR), and then w as contraction for W(rait) WROTE, carved the runes.

1

2

The reading proposed by me is:

ᚨᚠᛏᛒᛁᚼᛂᛂᚤᚦᚾᚱᛏᚱᛆᛒᚾ
ᚡᛏᚱᛒᛁᛒᛁᛂᚾᛒᚱᚾᛁ
ᚹᛒ

AFT ÆþINL., FAþUR, THURID
KÆMþU þIÆU þRUI.
HW. I(? = U(AIRWULFR) W(RAIT)|.
AFTER ÆTHINL., his-FATHER,
THURID NAMED (made) THIS THRUCH (stone-kist).
H . . . . W(rote the runes).

HELNÆS, FYN, DENMARK.

? DATE ABOUT A. D. 700—800.

(See C. C. Rafn, Antiqvarisk Tidsskrift, 8vo., 1858-60, Kjøbenhavn, p. 179-181; Prof. P. G. Thorsen, Danske Rune-mindesmærker, Vol. 1, Kjøbenhavn 1864, 8vo, p 335; G. Stephens, O. N. R. Monuments, p. 338.

Granite block, overgang (transitional) from the older to the later runes. Height about 6 feet 10 inches, greatest thickness about 2 feet. Runes from 4 to 5 inches high. But this block must originally have been nearly twice as broad. It was found March 18, 1860, on the land of the yeoman Lars Madsen to the right of the road from the north to Helnæs By, about 100 paces S. W. from a stoneset grave-chamber of far older date. When the stone was taken up it was found that a large piece had been long ago cloven away. The work-people unhappily now split it into 3 pieces, the 2 largest of which were used as gate-posts, and the third had the same destination. A couple of small pieces with runes were also broken off, and could not afterwards be found. The fragments were discovered and taken care of by Hr. Runge, the schoolmaster in Helnæs, and were examined by his late Majesty King Frederick VII in September 1860, who afterwards presented the whole to the O. N. Museum.

The 3 long lines are carved furrowwise. They show the O. N. rune ᚼ (u) twice, the O. N. ᛗ (m) once, and have ᚠ as the O. N. æ not as the Scandian O. Had o occurred in the risting, it would doubtless have been ᛉ. The lost letters are only 5 or 6, and these we can almost certainly restore. After the u must have come AN, thus HAN = HE, and then came UTI = ABROAD, or some other short word of a like kind. Beginning at the left line, and going up and down, the staves run:

ᚱᚼᚾᚾᚾᚠᛘᚼᛏᛏᛁᚼᛏᛏᛁᛏᚾᛃᛏ
ᚡᚾᚦᛁᛏᚠᛏᚤᚾᚦᚾᛗᚾᛏᛒᚱᚾᚦᚾᚱ
ᚼᚾᛏᚾᚼᛁᛏᛏᚱᚾᚤᛏᛏᚦ(ᚾᚼ . . . .)
ᚠᚾᛏᛁᛆᚡᛏᚦᛁ

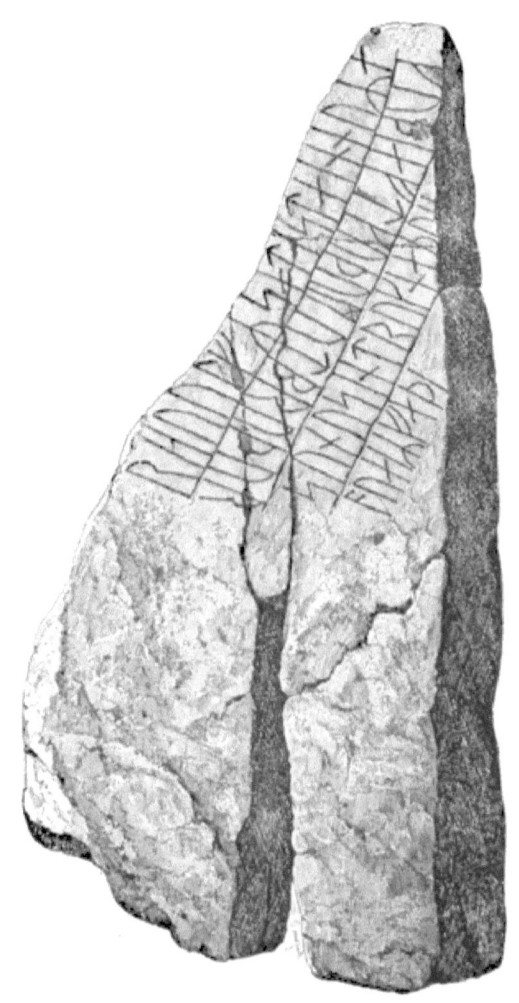

HELNÆS, FYEN.

SNOLDELEV, SEALAND.

KHUULFR SATI STAIN, NURA KUÞI, AFT KUÞI MUT,
BRUÞUR-SUNU SIN.   TRUKNAÞU (Han ? uti).
ÆUAIR FAÞI.

KHUULF SET this-STONE, of-the-NUR-men (or, of the NUR district) the-uirbi (Temple-chief and Civil
Magistrate) AFTER KUTHI MUT (= GUTHMUND), BROTHER-SON SIN (his). DROWNED (was-drowned)
(HE ? out [abroad]).

ÆUAIR FAYED (sculptured, carved, this stone and these runes).

There is a striking mixture of both early and late forms on this block. Thus we have SATI
and FAÞI, 3 s. p., with tho I, but also TRUKNAÞU, 3 s. p., with the older I'. Then there is STAIN,
ac. s. m., without the older final vowel, and SIN, also a similar ac. s. m., while at the same time
the antique vowel is preserved in the word SUNU, also ac. s. m. So we have the per-antique I'
in KUÞUMUT properly KUNÞUMUNT, the N being twice slurred.

Many runic monuments mention death by drowning.

This stone is remarkably illustrated by the Flemløse block. Not only do they both
belong to the same iland, Fyn, and the same folkland, of which Assens is the capital; but they
both seem to have concerned a mighty family of local dignity, civil and religious, the WULVES.
This monument is raised in memory of his brother-son by a chief named KHUULFR (= HELFR-
WULFR); the Flemløse block was inscribed to a magnate called KUULFR (= HEL FR-WULFR). Both
RUULF and KHUULF had the important office and title of GUTHI, and in the same district; each
was NURA GUTHI. And both ulila close with the same work-phrase. The one ends with ÆUAIR
FAÞI, the other with FUÆIR FAAÞU. Both are heathen overgang-stones, and perhaps the KHUULFR
of the one and the RUULFR of the other were *one and the same man*.

SNOLDELEV, SEALAND, DENMARK.

? DATE ABOUT A. D. 700—800.

(See Abrahamson, Skule Thorlacius, Børge Thorlacius «Den Snoldelevske Runesteen», Antiqvariske Annaler, 8vo. Kjøben-
havn 1812. Vol. 1, p 278-322; F. Magnusen, Antiqv. Annaler, 1820, Vol 3, p 304 ? A Rahamo, p 415, 457—65,
Liljegren, Run-Urkunder, Nr. 1474; J H. Bredsdorff, Biage ou Idun, København 1810, Vol. 3, p 5r2- 16; N M Petersen,
Danmarks Historie i Hedenold, 8vo, anden Udgave, Kjøbenhavn 1855, Vol. 3, p 272-3; C. C. Rafn, Inscription Runique
du Pirre, 8vo Copenhagen 1856, p. 186; Thorsen, De danske Runemindesmærker, Vol 1, p 13; G. Stephens, Old-
Northern Runic Monuments, p 345.)

Found on the Syla-how, only 1 Danish mile from Kallerup, near the close of the last
century. The whole Snoldelev district, in Thune Hundred, Roskilde Shire, has been very rich in
mighty antiquities. This one, a granitous graystone about 4 feet long, 2 feet 3 broad and 2½ inches
deep, was found *inside* the barrow to which it belonged. It came to the Round Tower in 1812.
Now that it has been flitted to the Museum the top can be seen, and here I have found a deep
round hole or «Cups», one of the holy symbols of the Stone Age. This was therefore a holy or
funeral block even at that early period, and was used again for the same purpose in the Iron
Age. Of this we have other examples. See this subject learnedly discust in Sir J. Y. Simson's

splendid quarto: «Archaic Sculpturings of Cups, Circles &c. upon Stones and Rocks in Scotland, England, & other Countries», Edinburgh 1867.

But this block is also remarkable in another way. Above the runes, on the left, are 3 Horns in the shape of the Triskele, here doubtless THE MARK OF THOR. On the right is the Flanged Thwarts or pre-Christian 4-angled cross, here doubtless THE MARK OF WODEN. See hereon Dr. Müller's admirable treatise «Religiøse Symboler», 4to, Kjøbenhavn 1864.

The rune ᛉ is here ᚼᚴᚼᚢ, as on so many of the oldest stones. Three-fourths of the last stave (ᛉ) is broken away, but there is no doubt of the letter. The olden ᚻ is still used for ᚼ.

ᚢ SALHAUKUM remains after 1000 years. It is the present hamlet of SALBY, SALLOW or SALHOH.

ᚱᚢᚾᚢᛁᛚᛏᛋᚢᛏᛁᚾ · ᛋᚢᚾᛁᚴ · ᚱᚢᚺᛁᛚᛏᛋ · ᚦᚢᛚᛁᚴ · ᚠᚢᛋᚱᚺᛁᛁᚢᚱᚢ(ᛉ)

KUNU‸ILTS ST‸IN, SUNAR RUHALTS, PULAR O SALHAUKU(M).

KUNUELT'S STONE, SON of-RUHALT, THYLE (Speaker) ON the-SALHOWS.

Between the 2 first words the S is *taken twice*, in the runic manner, to save space and trouble.

The exact meaning of the word ᚦᚢᛚ(ᚱ), everywhere so scarce, is not known. It may have signified either a wordly or a ghostly officer, a Priest or a Magistrate. I have since found it on the Hunterston Brooch.

GLENSTRUP, NORTH JUTLAND.
? DATE ABOUT A. D. 800—900.

(See Worm's Monumenta, p. 284; Antiqvariske Annaler, Vol. 1. Kjøbenhavn 1812, 8vo, p. 129; N. M. Petersen, Danmarks Historie i Hedenold, 2den Udgave, 8vo, Vol. 3. Kjøbenhavn 1855, p. 279; Liljegren, Run-urkunder, Nr. 1500; Rafn, Piece, p. 288.)

Worm informs us that this stone was formerly in the southern side of Glenstrup Church, but that the peasants said it had fallen down from the top of a barrow nearby, called *Auinar Høj*, and that a spring not far off was called *Thoro's Well*. They added that this chieftain *Thoro* had sacrificed his son to the Gods, and that thereupon this healing water had burst forth. In Christian times the Well, like the Church, was dedicated to *the 3 Maries*, retaining its healing virtues. After having been transported to the Danish capital, this sill (pillar) was one of the 3 which escaped the fire, and was transferred to the Round Tower, whence it came to the Runic Hall.

This dark granite block, from Glenstrup in Nørre Hald Hundred, Drønningborg Shire, Arhus See, is excessively antique. Its greatest height is about 5 feet, its greatest breadth nearly 3 feet. The surface is very much worn and some of the runes very faint, but the whole is legible

KIRKEBØ, FÆROES.

with a little patience. The letters are about 6 inches high. They are carved in a nearly square frame or cartouche.

The inscription, which begins at the bottom on the left, runs:

ᚦᚢᚱᛁᛆ : ᚱᛁᛋᛈᛁ : ᚼᛏᛁᛏ : ᚦᛆᛏᛋᛁ : ᛁᚠᛏᛁᛆ : ᚴᚢᛏᛏᚱ :

ᚠᛆᚦᚢᚱ : ᛋᛁᛏ :

þᵁᴿᴵᴿ ᴿᴵˢᴾᴵ ˢᵀᴵᴺ þᴬᴺˢᴵ ᴵᶠᵀᴵᴿ ᴷᵁᴺᴬᴿ,
ᶠᴬᴾᵁᴿ ˢᴵᴺ.

THᵁᴿᴵᴿ RAISED STONE THIS AFTER KUNAR,
FATHER SIN (his).

After ᴿᴵˢᴾᴵ, at about the middle of the band, is a deep horizontal flaw in the stone. This has hitherto been taken as a kind of ᴺ, while it has not been seen that the letter ᴺ (ᚼ) *is really on the stone*, before the following ᴛ, altho this ᴺ-rune is now very dim. But a paper cast will bring it plainly out.

· — ·· — ·· — ·

KIRKEBO, FÆROES.

† DATE ABOUT A. D. 800—900.

(See F Magnusen in Nordisk Tidsskrift for Oldkyndighed, Vol. 2, 1833, p 319, and in Runamo 1841, p 349, 555, 652; Th. G. Repp in Kjøbenhavnsposten 1838, p. 1259; G. Stephens, O. N. Runic Monuments, p. 729.)

Is of the dark igneous stone called Dolerite, and is engraved 1—3rd of the full size. Was found in 1833, in digging up the foundations of an old house in Kirkebo, the see of the Færoe bishops in former times, on the iland Strømø, and was sent to the capital by Governor Pløyen. In spite of previous efforts I take it to have been hitherto undeciphered. I think the inscription to be complete, the fragment being the top of the stone, and that the runes clearly are — if carefully examined and copied as tho they were not reverst:

ᛁᚵᛏᛁᛉᛁᚋᛁᛁᚾᛁᚴᛁᚠᛏᛁᚾᛁᛁᚱᛁᚾᛁ

ˢᴬᵀᴵ ᴹᴵᴴ ᵁᴵᴷ ᵁᶠᵀ ᵁᴺᴵᴿᵁ.

SET ME UIK AFTER UNIRU.

Here we have a formula excessively rare — SET ME —; the mansname UIK in the nominative without any nom. mark; and an example of the mansname UNRU with the ᴺ still left, as on the Swedish Ångvrota stone.

The staves are turned round, and read from right to left. This was seen and pointed out by my foregangers.

STENDERUP (or ELTANG), NORTH JUTLAND, DENMARK.

? DATE ABOUT A. D. 800—900.

(See G. Stephens Old-Northern Runic Monuments, p. 562.)

As we see, only the half of this grey-stone funeral block is left to us. The lower part is gone. But most happily the piece before us — here carefully engraved 1—4th of the full size — is so far complete that *the whole inscription is preserved*. Not one letter is absent. It belongs to that ancient class of monuments on which the runes are written within a frame or cartouche, and the whole of this frame-line remains except a little bit at the right corner.

It is also another piece of good luck that this runic block was not barbarously destroyed as soon as found, which is too often the case. Thro the efforts of Land-inspector Lieut. Müller, Rector Kinch of Ribe, and Mr. Flensborg the proprietor of the estate on which it was discovered, it has been duly taken care of, and Mr. Flensborg has now generously given it to the Old-Northern Museum. State-Councilor Worsaae has been indefatigable in watching over it, and I have to thank him for the information he has gathered concerning it.

It was found early in the year 1866 on a bit of wild land close to a beck, just south of Mr. Flensborg's mansion, about a mile and a quarter Danish north of Kolding, Veile Amt, in the village of North-Stenderup and Parish of Eltang. From the name of the Parish, it may also be called the Eltang stone.

The 2nd and 3rd letters are *sam-staves* (2 or more letters on the *same stave*), and the 1st, 4th and 5th must also be lookt upon as cut in half, taken twice. We have such sam-staves on many other monuments. Consequently the word ᚢᛏᛁᚾ is redd both as the *first* word and also as the *last* word in this short sentence, I standing for ᛁ and ᛁ, ᛒ for ᚦ and ᛒ (o and o), ᛒ for ᚦ and ᚦ (TH and TH), I for ᛁ and ᛁ, and ᛏ (here as so often elsewhere elegant for ᚾ — N) for N and N. The reading will therefore be:

ᛁᚠᚦᛁᛏᚦᛁᚡᛁᛁᚦᚦᛁᛏ

ᚢᛏᛁᚾ ᚦᛁᚲᛁ ᚢᛏᛁᚾ.

may-WOTHIN THIU (take, receive) WOTHIN!

As the oldest form of this name was WOᚦIN, but which in many dialects was softened to OᚦIN, I look upon the ᛁ as a local Jutlandish prefix, as in so many other words. Should we suppose the first and last ᛁ to be a mark only and not a letter, making the name OTHIN instead of WOTHIN, the meaning will be the same.

The first WOTHIN is seemingly the name of the God, the second the name of a man — a servant or priest or victim offered in sacrifice to that God. Therefore the funeral block recommends the deceast (whether a ·human offering· or no) to the protection and heavenly hospitality of the Lord of Walhall. Thus, either *at his natural death*, or on occasion of some public calamity or to procure victory *at his being offered as a noble victim*, the dead man's clan or family inscribed

O WODEN, RECEIVE THY SERVANT WODEN!

Scandinavia has 2 runic stones bearing the name of the God THUR. This is the only one yet found bearing the name of the God ODIN.

STENDERUP, NORTH-JUTLAND.

TRYGGEVÆLDE, SEALAND. (A).

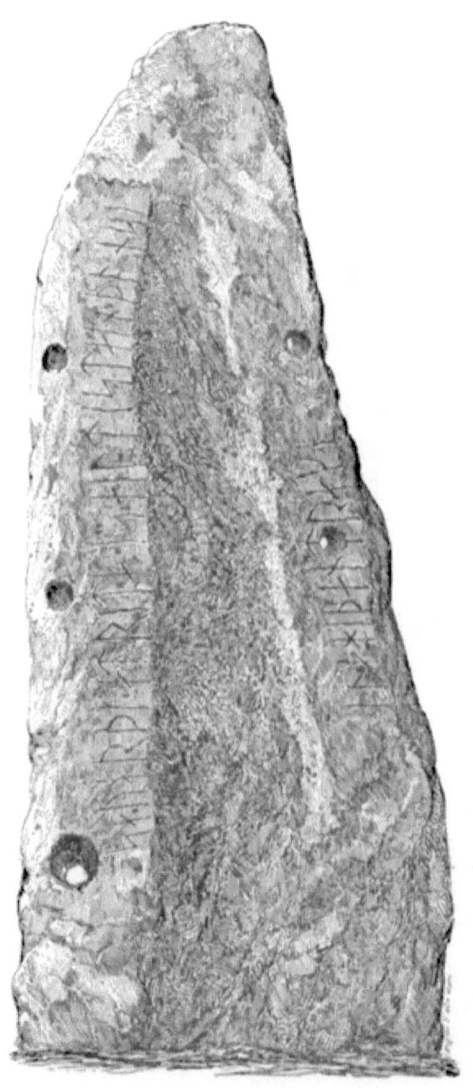

TRYGGEVÆLDE, SEALAND. (B).

TRYGGEVÆLDE, SEALAND.

? DATE ABOUT A. D. 800—900.

(See Bonaventura Vulcanius, De litteris et lingua Getarum sive Gothorum, 8vo, Lugd. Bat. 1597, p 45. Lyschander, De Danske Kongers Slectebog, Fol. Kjøbenhavn 1622, p 145; Olaus Wormius, De Monumento Tryggeveldensi, Hafniæ 1636, 4to & Monumenta p. 105—117; Prof. Nyerup in det Skandinaviske Litteraturselskabs Skrifter, 8vo, Vol 8, Kjøbenhavn 1900, p 404—54, R & Rask, idem Vol. 8, p 435—47 & Samlede Afhandlinger, 8vo, Vol 5, København 1834, p 411 —23; Prof. Werlauff, in Nordisk Tidsskrift for Oldkyndighed, 8vo, Vol 1, Kjøbenhavn 1832, p 295, Liljegren, Run-Ur-kunder, Nr. 1468; C. C. Rafn, Inscription Runique de Pirée, 8vo, Copenhague 1856, p. 185—7, G. Stephens O N Runic Monuments, p. 807—15.)

This venerable monument first attracted public attention in 1566, when Poul Vobis, Governor of Tryggevælde Castle, removed it (? from the Kis How) to the Castle-yard. Thus it came from Little Tårnby, Hårløv Parish, Faxe Hundred, Præstø Shire. Probably at this flitting the holes were bored thro it, for the ropes by which the oxen dragged it along. Between 1654 and 1658 it was again moved, this time by Christian Skeel of Fusinge, Governor of Tryggevælde, to his seat at Valle. While here it was again copied by Prof. Nyerup, and his has hitherto been the best facsimile. In 1810 it was sent to the capital and placed in Trinity churchyard, where it remained till it came to the Museum in March 1867. My drawings were made in 1864.

This hard gray-stone block is about 9 feet high, 4 at broadest, and averages 1 foot in thickness. Some of the staves are so much injured as to be made out only after a long and patient examination.

I take the AUK SKAIÞ to have been added by the artist at the announcement by the Lady RAGNHILD that she would raise that as well as the other grave-marks, and that their place is after the words AUK KARÞI HAUK ÞÆNSI. I also suppose that she was twice married, and that the Glavendrup stone was raised by her to her other husband.

I begin with the 3rd line, then take the 2nd at its left (with the 1st after HAUK ÞÆNSI), ending with the last word AUFT, then the 4th and 5th, and end with the formula on the other side.

ᚱᛅᚴᚾᚺᛁᛚᛏᚱ · ᛋᚢᛋᛏᛁᛦ · ᚢᛚᚠᛋ · ᛋᛅᛏᛁ · ᛋᛏᛅᛁᚾ · ᚦᛅᚾᛋᛁ ·
ᛅᚢᚴ · ᚴᛅᚱᚦᛁ · ᚼᛅᚢᚴ · ᚦᛅᚾᛋᛁ · ᛅᚢᚴ · ᛋᚴᛅᛁᚦ · ᚦᛅᛋᛁ · ᛅᚢᚠᛏ
· ᚴᚢᛏᚢᛚᚠ · ᚢᛅᚱ · ᛋᛁᚾ · ᚴᛚᛅᛘᚢᛚᛅᚾ · ᛘᛅᚾ · (ᛋᚢ)ᚾ · ᛏᛅᛁᚱᛓᛁᛋ ·
ᚠᛅᛁ(ᛦ) · ᚢᛅᚱᚦᛅ · ᚾᚢ
ᚠᚢᛏᛁᛦ · ᚦᛅᛁ · ᛒᛅᛏᚱᛁ
ᛋᛅ · ᚢᛅᚱᚦᛁ · ᛅᛏ · ᚱᛁᛏᛅ · ᛁᛋ · ᛅᛁᛚᛏᛁᛋᛏᛅᛁᚾ · ᚦᛅᚾᛋᛁ · ᛁᚠᛅ
ᛏᛁᚦᛅᚾ · ᛏᚱᛅᚴᛁ

RAKNHILTR, SUSTIR ULFS, SATI STAIN ÞÆNSI, AUK KARÞI HAUK ÞÆNSI AUK SKAIÞ ÞANSI, AUFT KUNULF, UAR SIN, KLÆMULAN MAN, (SU')N NAIRBIS.

FAIR UARÞA NU
FUTIR ÞÆI BATRI.

SA UARÞI AT RITA IS AILTI STAIN ÞÆNSI, IFA TIÞAN TRAKI!

RAKNHILT, SISTER of-ULF, SET STONE THIS, EKE (and) GARED (made) HOW (gravemound, low) THIS EKE SKETH (? Ship-setting, Stone-setting) THIS, AFTER KUNULF, WER (husband) HIS (her), a-GLAMROUS (eloquent, illustrious) MAN, the-SON of-NAIRBI.

FEW WORTH NOW
FED (born) THE BETTER!
(— Few are now born better than he.)

SA (he) WORTH (become) AT (to) A-MITI (an outlaw) AS (who) shall-WELT (overturn) STONE THIS,
OR BETHEN (hence) shall-DRAW-it)!

(— Let him be an Outlaw who casts down this stone, or who drags it hence for other use or for
the grave of another man!)

Stones found elsewhere support the above translation of SKAIÞ ÞANSI.

The closing threat is also on other monuments, and is paralleled by expressions in
the old *barbaric* grave-dooms.

ASFERG, NORTH JUTLAND, DENMARK.

¶ DATE ABOUT A. D. 900—1000.

(See Antiqvariske Annaler, Vol 1. Kjøbenhavn 1812, p. 352. Vol 4, 1827, p 523; C. C. Rafn, Pérec, p. 209; G. Stephens.
Old-Northern Runic Monuments, p. 637.)

This granite block is about 3 feet 7 inches high by about 2 feet 3 broad. Runes about
5 inches high. It was found in 1795 in or on a barrow in Asferg Parish, Nørrehald Hundred,
Randers Amt. The name of the exact mark or open land where the grave-mound stood is
Eistrup Mill Mark, and hence it has sometimes been called the Eistrup stone. It was used as
a gang-block, outside the door of the Mill. But in 1810 it was *frithed* — purchased and protected
— by the Danish Antiquarian Commission, and in 1825 was sent in to the capital and placed in
the Round Tower.

When the runes were first made public in 1827, the last 5 staves were not deciphered.
Rafn gave 4 of these correctly, but could not read the last which is ᛏ (N). Observe the form
here given to the N. We cannot decide whether ᛏ here signifies the older æ or the later o. To
be on the safe side, I have given it as o. — The inscription reads ploughingwise, and is heathen.
It has the striking ac. s. masc. KUÞRU for the usual KUÞAN. In other words, the R has been
retained from the nominative or else dialectically added (of which we have other examples), while
the N is nasalized and silent, in this process the A becoming U. The runes read:

: ᚦᚢᚱᚴᛁᛆ : ᛏᚢᚴᚨ : ᛋᚢᚾᛁ : ᚱᛁᛒᚢᛁ : ᛒᛏᛁᛏ · ᚦᛁᛏᚺᛁ : ᛁᛈᛏᛁᛆ :
ᛘᚢᛚᛏ : ᛒᚱᚢᚦᚱ : ᛋᛁᛏ : ᛆᛆᚱᚦᛏ : ᚴᚢᚦᚱᚢ : ᚦᛁᛏ

ÞURKIR, TUKA SUN, RISÞI STIN ÞONSI EFTIR MULA, BRUÞR SIN, HARÞO KUÞRU ÞIN.

THURKIR, TUKI'S SON, RAISED STONE THIS AFTER MULA, BROTHER SIN (his), A-HARD (very) GOOD
THANE (soldier, hero, chief).

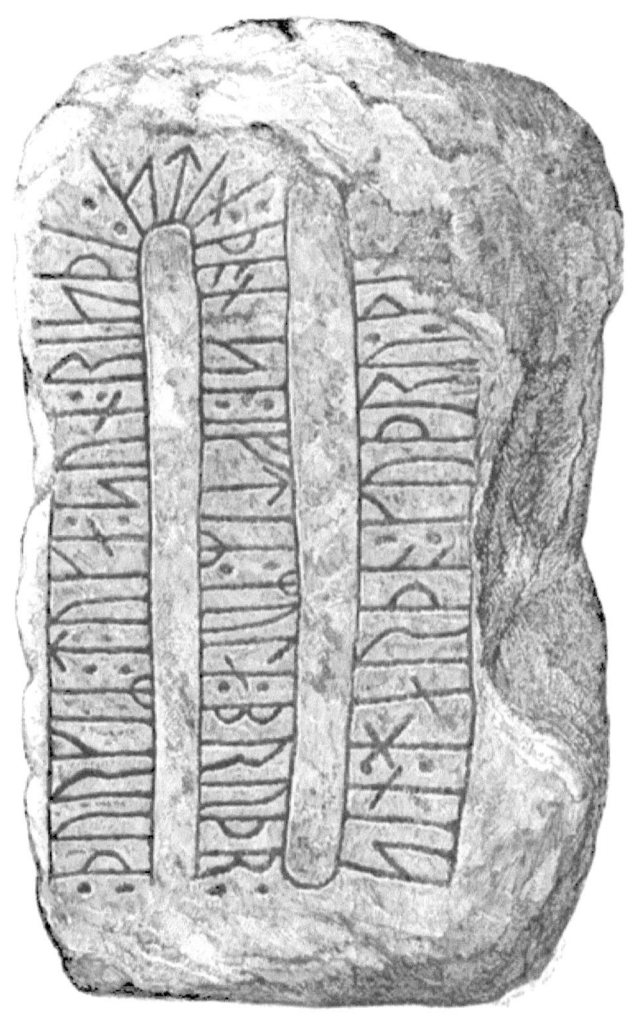

ASFERG, NORTH-JUTLAND.

BREGNINGE, LOLLAND.

? DATE ABOUT A. D. 900—1000.

(See Wormii Monumenta Danica, Fol Hafniæ 1643, p. 261; Liljegren, Run-Urkunder, Nr. 1490.)

Worm states that this granite block, which is excessively rough and broken, was formerly in the north wall of the churchyard of Bregninge, to which it was brought from a neighboring barrow. His engraving gives the stone as standing, so that the runic lines are perpendicular, and his copy of the text is correct. Only he mistakenly has ᛁ (i), instead of ᚦ (þ.), in the word HAKLAKS. Previous to its removal to the Museum, this monument was in Trinity churchyard. Its size is about 5 feet 3 inches high by 4 feet 10 inches broad, the runes about 11 inches high. But the writing is much defaced, here and there scarcely legible, from the fishermen at Nysted quay having for a long time beaten their dry fish upon the inscribed surface.

The runes are in 5 lines, thus:

```
:ᚾᚢᛏ�★·
:ᛏᚢᚤᛏ:ᛏᛏᚤᛚᛏᚤᚾ
:ᚾᚢᛏ:ᚾᛁᛏ:ᛏᛏᚤ:
:ᛏᚾᛏ:ᚤᛏᛦᛁ:ᚤᚢᛒᚤ:
:ᚦᚢᚾᛁ:ᛏᚤᛏ:ᛏᚢᚤᛏ·
```

I take the runes in the order line 4, 5, 3, 2, 1, and translate:

ASA KARÞI KUBL ÞUSI AFT TUKA, SUN SIN, AOK TUKA-HAKLAKS SU'NAR.

ASA GARED (made) CUMBELS THESE AFTER TUKI, SON SIN (her), EKE (and) TUKI-HAKLAK'S SONS. (— These grave-marks (the stone and the Low) were made in memory of TUKI by ASA, his mother, and by his brothers, the sons of TUKI-HAKLAKI).

Thus ASA was a widow, her husband (TUKI-HAKLAK) being dead.

Bregninge or Breininge is in Musse Herred and Ålholm Amt.

EGÅ, NORTH JUTLAND.

? DATE ABOUT A. D. 900—1000.

(See Antiqvariske Annaler, 8vo, Vol. 2, Kjøbenhavn 1815, p 355, Vol. 3, 1820, p. 382; Werlauff, Nordisk Tidsskrift for Oldkyndighed, 8vo, Vol 2, Kjøbenhavn 1834, p. 242—7; N M. Petersen, Danmarks Historie i Hedenold, ed. 2, 8vo, Vol. 3. Kjøbenhavn 1855, p. 279.)

Of light granite. Upwards of 4 feet high; greatest breadth 2 feet 3 inches. Runes from 8 to 4 inches high. Was found in 1814 in the stone fence at Egå, Egå Parish, Randers Shire. Before this was dug up from a bank called Brobjergbakke, on the left of Egå bridge,

2

and has doubtless been on or in one of the neighboring grave-mounds. The top bit was broken away when Worlauff's essay and woodcut appeared, but has since been discovered, so that this monument is now complete. But at the beginning a part of the AL has been smasbt off, and a small piece is wanting on which was a bit of the IS in MISÞU. Otherwise the whole is plain enough.

There is no difficulty in the risting, which runs round the stone, from left to right, in 3 lines:

ᚨᛚᚠᚴᛁᛚ ᛬ ᚢᚴ ᛬ ᚦᛅᚾ ᛬ ᛋᚢᚾᛁᛅ ᛫ ᚱ(ᛁᛋ)ᚦᚢ ᛬ ᛋᛏᛁᚾ ᛬ ᚦᛅᛋᛁ ᛬
ᛁᚹᛏ ᛬ ᛘᛅᚾᛅ ᛬ ᛋᛁᚾ ᛬ ᚠᚱᛁᛋᛏᛅ ᛬ ᚦᛅᚾ ᛫ ᚢᛅᛋ ᛫ ᛚᛅᚾᛏᛁᚱᚦᛁ ᛬
ᚴᛁᛏᛁᛚᛋ ᛬ ᚦᛁᚾ ᛬ ᛏᚢᚱᚢᚾᛅ ᛬

ALFKIL, ᴜᴋ HANS SUNIR RISÞU STIN ÞASSI IFT MANA, SIN FRINTA, ÞAN'S UAS LANTIRÞI KITILS ÞIN NURUNA.

ALFKIL EKE HIS SONS RAISED STONE THIS AFTER MANI, HIS (their) FRIEND (Kinsman), THAN (him) AS (who) WAS LANDWARD (land-warden, bailiff, governor) of-KITIL THE NORRANE (Norseman, Norwegian.)

In LANTIRÞI we cannot determine whether the compound is from LAND and HIRÞI or LAND and URÞI. — ÞIN is the gen. singl. masc. of ÞE, THE.

KIRKEBY, FALSTER.
† DATE ABOUT A. D. 900—1000.

(See Prof. Werlauff. and Bredsdorff's drawing, in Antiqvariske Annaler, 8vo, Vol. 1, 1812, p. 74—81. and Tab. 3, Fig. 3. Liljegren, Run-Urkunder, Nr. 1184; G. Stephens, O. N. Runic Monuments, p. 739, 3.)

Whence this block originally came is unknown. It was formerly in the northwest wall of Sønder (South) Kirkeby church, in Sønder Herred, Nykøbings Amt, Falster, where it did duty as a building-block. Thence it was removed by the Danish Antiquarian Commission in 1811 to the Round Tower. It is nearly square, of reddish quartzose granite, about 2 feet 2 inches high by 2 feet 3½ broad, and is more than one foot thick.

The inscription begins on the left of the undermost line, and thence each line above. The 1st letter of the 1st word is injured, but sufficient remains to show that it was ⟨o⟩, and thus the name was the common OSUR, older form ANSUAR. The close of the risting is in sam-staves. The last letters in the top line being KU, the first sam-stave group gives RU, the second IA, the third LANT. In this last cluster we have — as so often — the «runic elegance» ⟨N⟩ for ⟨A⟩ and ⟨A⟩ for ⟨N⟩. The ⟨T⟩ is plain. The whole word was thus KURUTLIANT, for KIRUTLIANTI, the I of the dative omitted as is so frequently the case. KURULILANT (N. t. KIRJALA-LAND), CARELIA-LAND), was the folkland north and northeast of the Gulf of Finland, now — with more limited borders — called KARELEN.

KIRKEBY, FALSTER.

Above the whole, as far as the narrow space would allow, is carved the figure of a Ship — OSUR'S War-galley.

The rugged bit of the stone across the sam-staves and the ship *has never been carved upon*. It was too hard and jagged.

We thus get:

ᚠᛋᚢᚱ : ᛋᛅᛏᛁ : ᛋᛏᛁᚾ : ᚦᛁᚾᛋᛁ : ᚼᛅᚠᛏ : ᛆᛋᚴᛚ : ᛒᚱᚢᚦᚱ :
ᛋᛁᚾ : ᛁᛅᚾ : ᚢᛅᚱᚦ : ᛏᚢᚦᚱ : ᚭ : ᚴᚢᚱᚱᛚᛁᛚᛅᚾᛏ

(O)SUR SATI STIN ÞINSI HAFT OSKL, BRUÞUR SIN, IAN UARÞ TUÞR O KURULLANT.

OSUR SET STONE THIS AFTER OSKL (= OSKITIL), BROTHER SIN (his), WHO WORTH DEAD (fell, was slain), ON (in) KURULL-LAND (Carelia).

Thus the Danish low was a Cenotaph, for the dead hero had fallen in Finland.

Wiking (naval adventure) to *Finland* is mentioned on several *Swedish* stones. Should my translation be correct, this is the first instance hitherto found on any *Danish* runic block.

TIRSTED, LOLLAND.

? DATE ABOUT A. D. 900—1000.

(See Wormii Monumenta, p. 267; R. Nyerup, Verzeichniss der in Dänemark 1824 noch vorhandenen Runensteine, 8vo, Copenhagen 1824; Prof. Rask, l. c. p. 41–52 & Samlede Afhandlinger, Vol. 3, p. 438–445; Liljegren, Run-Urkunder Nr 1492; N. M. Petersen, Danmarks Historie i Hedenold, Vol. 3, p. 277; Hafn. Pirre, p. 180–193; G. Stephens, O. N. Runic Monuments, p. 798–802.)

Of quartzose granite, 7 feet high, greatest breadth about 6 feet 7 inches. The surface is in its natural state (has never been tooled), and this has influenced the artist in cutting the runes. This stone also has several artificial small cup-like holes, from the stone age, as is the case with some other runic blocks. See the Snoldelev stone. This monument has suffered greatly, but all the runes can still be made out. It is remarkable for 2 examples of the article ÞA, THE, prefixt, as in English.

We know not from what tumulus this minne-stone came. It is first mentioned by Worm as »adorning the southern side of the churchyard in the village of Tirsted», Fugelse Hundred. Next it was taken to Nysted, in 1815 was removed to the capital (Trinity churchyard), and came in March 1867 to the Museum.

My facsimile, the result of great care, differs in various places from any hitherto given, and I hope is absolutely correct. Beginning at the bottom of the 1st line on the right, and then taking each line to the left, the inscription is as follows:

ᛆᚾᚱᛅᚦᚱ · ᛅᚢᚴ · ᚼᛁᛚᛏᚢᛚᚠᛦ · ᚱᛅᛁᚾᚦᚢ · ᚾᛏᛅᛁᛋᚦᛅᛋᛋᛁ · ᛅᚠᛏ
ᚠᚱᛆᚦᛅ · ᛒᚱᛆᚾᛏᛁ · ᚾᛁᛋ · ᚾᛁᛆ · ᛁᛅᚾ · ᚼᛅᛋ ᚢᛅᚾᚦᛆ · ᚠᛆᛁᛋᚴ · ᚢᛅᛁᛦᛅ ·
ᛁᛅᛋ · ᚼᛅᛋᚢᛅᚱᚦ ᛏᛅᚢᚦᚱ · ᛆ · ᚾᚢᛆᚦᛁᛅᚢᚦᚢ · ᛅᚢᚴ · ᚢᛅᚾ ·
ᚠᚢᚱᚴᛁ · ᛁᛒᚱᛁᚴᛁᚾ · ᛚᛆᚦᛁ · ᚦᛆ · ᛅᛚᛁᛦᚢᛁᚴᛁᚴᛅᛦ

ÆSRAFR AFK HILTULFR RAISÞU STAIN ÞANSI AFT FRÆÞA FRLNTI SIN, SIII.

IAN HAN UAS Þ:E VÆINK UAIRA.

IAN HAN UARÞ TAUÞR Æ SUÆÞIAUÞU, AUK UAS FURKI I FRIKIS LÆÞI, Þ:E ALIR UIKIKAR.

ÆSRATH EKE (and) HILTULF RAISED STONE THIS AFTER FROD (wise, prudent, noble, illustrious) FRIEND (kinsman) SIN (their), SIII.

IN (but) HE WAS THE FOEING (foeman, terror, scourge) of-WERR (men).

IN (but) HE WORTH DEAD (fell, perisht) IN SWITHIOD (Sweden), EKE (and) WAS LEADER IN FRIKIR'S LITH (fleet, forces), THE HALE (hero) of-the-WIKING (Wiking-foray, war-expedition).

We have parallels of the words and formulas VÆINK, FURKI I LÆÞI (LIÞS FURKI), ALIR (HALIR, HALR) UIKIKAR (nom. UIKINK), on other stones.

I believe that this and the Seddinge block (which latter has an example of the infinitive in -AN) were both raised to the same hero.

The great expedition headed by FRIKIR (or FRAIKIR), probably to Finland, Russia and the south, is mentioned on other runic monuments dating from this same century.

BÅRSE, SEALAND.

? DATE ABOUT A. D. 1000—1100.

(See Antiquariske Annaler, Vol. 4, Kjøbenhavn 1827, p. 353.)

Only a fragment. Was found in 1822 among the stones in the street of Bårse, Præstø, and was given to the Museum by Pastor Heusemann. These street-stones were said to have been taken, in former times, from an old «Waldemarsvej» (King's highroad) in the neighborhood. Is apparently *the end* of the inscription. Of the 4 remaining letters one is a clear ↑ (R), a «stung» or dotted rune, and thus the block has not been excessively forn.

But below is a bind-rune, one of whose 2 staves is the Old-Northern Þ (w), the other is ↑ (H). Thus we have here a parallel to the Vordingborg stone. As the one has ᚼᛈ (HW), so the other has ᚠ (HW). As on the Vordingborg block so here, the w doubtless stands for WHAIT or WHITI or WHITADE, or however the word may then and there have sounded.

This ᚠ cannot have been a monogram of the name of Christ, as has hitherto been said, for this monogram came in about the 4th century but died out in the 5th; and among the *couple of thousands* of rune-stones known to us *not one* has any such monogram.

All then now left of this overgang-block is:

— — — — — — — —
— — — — — — — — — — ᚠᚼS(?i)
ᚠ

(? After N. N., ... his (or her), N. N. raised (or let raise) stone THIS.
H . . . . . WROTE-the-runes.

Prof. L. Müller has learnedly treated the question of the Christian monograms in Kgl. Danske Vidensk. Forhandlinger, 8vo. No. 6, 1866.

BÅRSE, SEALAND.

FRODEBO, FÆROES.

? DATE ABOUT A. D. 1000–1100.

(See Fin Magnusen's Runamo, p. 557.)

Found in 1840 at Frodebo, Sudero, by a peasant digging in the earth. Sent to the Museum by Governor Pløyen. Is of Færoe basalt, about 2½ feet long, 12 inches broad above and 11 below, and about 10 inches thick. On the upper half is carved a double-lined *Cross pattée*, the stem a little longer than the arms. There is no inscription. Here and there, however, a later hand has scratcht-in a small rune or two or a bind-rune, within the arms of the rood.

SANDBY, SEALAND.

? DATE ABOUT A. D. 1000–1100.

(See Wormii Monumenta, Fol., p. 122.)

When Worm gave his woodcut of the 1st side only of this broken stone it was in the quire-wall of the church at Sandby, Tybierg Hundred, Sealand. The other side was therefore hidden. But it was afterwards taken out and sent to the Round Tower, where the inscription on the other side became visible. It is only about half the original block, and nearly 1-third of the risting on each face is lost. As we now have it, this piece is about 5 feet greatest height, 2 feet average breadth, 4 to 12 inches in thickness, staves from 3 to 6 inches long. The runes are:

FIRST SIDE, ONE TREBLE BAND AND ONE DOUBLE BAND.

ᛋᚢᛚᚠᛆ : ᚱᛂᛋᛏ(........ᚱ)ᚦᛁ : ᛒᚱᚢ : ᚦᛁᛋᛁ : ᛁᚠᛏ : ᚦᚢᚱᛁᛚᛋ :
ᛒᚱᚦᚢᚱ : ᛋᛁᚿ(.......)ᛁ : ᛋᛒᛆᛚᚴᛁᚢᛋᚢ : ᛂᚨᚠᛏᛁ : ᛋᚢᛋᚢᚱ :
ᚠᛆᚦᚢᚱ...

SECOND SIDE, ONE TREBLE BAND.

ᛁᛉᚢᚿᛋᛆ(ᚿ............)ᛁᚠ · ᚢᛁᛏᚱᛁᚴ · ᛋᚢᛋᛁ · ᛁᛦ · ᚢᛆᚿ · ᛋᛁᛚ...

This risting has never been redd. I propose as follows, the last 4 lines being in stave-rime:

SULFA REST(?i stain auk kar)þi BRU ÞISI IFT ÞURILS BRUÞUR SIN (? kuþan, auk set)i SKALKIUSU ECFTI MUSUR, FAÞUR (? sin).

I MUN SAN (? uera,
meþ stain bauir liuf.
UITRIK SUSI
IR VAN SIL(fa)!

SULFA RAISED (stone-this eke gared) BRIDGE THIS AFTER THIRILS, BROTHER SIN (his) (? good, eke
set)-it SHALKIUSU AFTER SUSUR, FATHER (sin · · her).

> AYE MUN (shall, will) SOUTH (true) WARE (be),
> MITH (while, long as) STONE HATH LIFE,
> WORTHING (glory) SU (that)
> AS (which) WAN (gained) SILFA!

My translation of the last formula is supported by that which is found on the Tillitse
stone, Lolland :

> E MUN STANTA,
> MED STEN LIFIR,
> UTHINT SU
> IAR UAN ESKIL.

> AYE MUN (shall, will) STAND,
> MITH (while, long as) STONE LIVETH,
> WORTHING (glory) SU (that)
> AS (which) WAN (gained) ESKIL!

We know nothing of the famous heroes here commemorated, or what the WORTHING —
the endless honor — was which they had won.

As far as we can see, the stone was raised by living children, SULFA (SILFA), in memory
of his brother THIRILS, and the Lady SHALKIUSU in memory of her father SUSUR. But possibly
SHALKIUSU was not the sister of SULFA. THIRILS and SUSUR may have fallen together on some
expedition, and the brother of the one and the daughter of the other may have joined in raising
the common monument.

GIESINGHOLM, NORTH JUTLAND, DENMARK.

? DATE ABOUT A. D. 1134, 1135.

(See Worsaae Monumenta, p. 285. Antiqvariske Annaler, Vol 4, Kjøbenhavn 1827, p. 205, G. Stephens in Illustreret Tidende,
Kjøbenhavn, Sept. 1, 1867, p 397.)

The oldest engraved copy of this Tombslab is that in Worm. It is very incorrect.
Somewhat better is the unpublisht drawing by Abildgaard, made in 1760 and now in the Archives
of the Old-Northern Museum. The stone itself was formerly in the Chapel of Giesingholm Castle,
South Hald Herred, and was given to the Antiquarian Commission in 1821 by Cancellirad Ras-
mussen, the then owner of Giesingholm. It was placed in the aisle of Trinity Church, and was
removed to the Museum in 1867. It is of dark granite, about 5 feet 2 inches long, 18½ inches
broad at top and 16 at bottom, and from 4 to 8 inches thick. In low relief it bears the figure of
a Bishop, standing and about to bless, his Episcopal Staff firmly graspt in his left hand. Below
is a horned Lamb, carrying on its left foot the Holy Rood. This is doubtless the usual ancient

GIESINGHOLM, NORTH-JUTLAND.

symbol of Christ and the Holy Cross, the great Christian emblem of salvation, and in fact answers
to the olden legend or motto: «Agnus Dei qui tollis peccata mundi, miserere nobis!»

By the assistance of Worm and Abildgaard, we can see what originally stood on the
stone where it is now injured. The inscription begins on the left edge at the top:

ᚦᚢᛚᚦ ᛬ ᚴᛆᚦᛁ ᛬ ᚦᛆᚼᛁ ᛬ ᚼᛖᚿᚠ ᛬ ᛆᚴᛆ ᛬ ᚦᛆᚱᛁᛆ ᛬ ᛆᛒᛁ ᛬ ᚼᚿᛁ ᛬ ᛚᛆᚼᛁ

ᚦᚢᛚᚦ ᛫ ᛫ ᛫ ᛫

THLÆTH OARED (made, let make, raised) THIS HWALF (hulling, vault, tomb) OVER THURO ABLÆ-
SON LANGE.

THLÆTH is apparently, the R elided,   the name commonly spelt THORTH. OAUF is a
Jutish slurring for WÆUF, HUALF, here as in O. English and O. Swedish masculine not neuter.

The foot end of this slab has never been inscribed, probably having at first stood near
to the church-wall.

The right side bore — and most of the runes can still be made out   :

᛬ ᚿᛁᚼ ᛬ ᛒᛁᚦᛁᛆᚤᛆᚱᛁ ᛬ ᛬ ᛌᛆᛁᚼᛆᚱ ᛬ ᛁᛁᚤᛘᛆᚠᚿ ᛬ ᚴᛆᛏᛁ

The ᛌ in the last word is a Roman N; the next letter is a bind, A and TH, as in ᚴ
(Y and L) in SYLI.

VIS, HEDIR, MARI, NAÞI! SYLI NIKLAOS KÆTI!

WIS (show, grant) HEDE-ye (beg, pray ye) O-MARY, NATHE (mercy, pity)! HIS-SOUL, may-Saint-
NICHOLAS OAIT (guard, keep, save, bless)!

The last edge, the short one at the head of the slab, has 8 letters, all Latin except
the ᚦ. The two central staves are ornamental in shape. I take the whole to be:

HORDERUS

apparently the name of the sculptor HORDER in a Latinized form. Thus equivalent to

HORDER CARVED THIS.

The THURO or THURE here commemorated was apparently the Bishop of Ribe, the only
Bishop in Denmark who bore that name. He fell in the battle of Fotvik or Fodvig in 1134, and
his body must have been privately buried at Giesingholm.

BRATTAHLID, GREENLAND.

? DATE ABOUT A. D. 1100 1200.

(See Antiquarisk Tidsskrift, 1858 60, p. 9.)

A broken bit of red sandstone, about 10 inches long by 9 broad and 2 thick. Runes
nearly 3 inches high, but very faint and worn. Only a letter or two is really distinct. This lafe
was found at Brattahlid, Igelikko fiord, in 1857, and was sent over by Dr. H. Rinck. We have
apparently the middle of the carving. The fragment begins with R, preceded by the lower part
of 4 letters, I think the word has been (AFTI)R, and that we may make out

.... R : (ᛁᛦᚼᚱ(ᚦ)) ....

... (ᚦᚾᚱ ᛁ ᚦᚦᚦ' ᛌ)ᛁᚱ · (ᛚ·) ....

.... (aftiᚢ (siᚴᛦᛦ)tᚢ) ....

(ᚠᛦᚱ ᚼᚨᚾᛌ), ᛁᚱ (ᛁ) ....

(N. N. raised this stone afte)ᚱ (siᚴᛦ ᛦ) .... (and after N. N. broTHER his), AS (who) IN ....
But I offer this reading with diffidence, the stone having suffered so much.

BRYNDERSLEV, NORTH JUTLAND. DENMARK.

? DATE ABOUT A. D. 1100—1200.

(See Worm, Monumenta Danica, Fol. p. 256; Prof. Rask. Antiqvariske Annaler, 8vo. Vol. 3, kjøbenhavn 1820, p. 83—92
(& Samlede Afhandlinger, Vol. 3, p. 428—431); Ligrøren, Ron-Urkunder, Nr. 1934; C. C. Rafn, Parte, p. 229; G. Stephens, Old-Northern Runic Monuments, p. 660—60.)

This stone was formerly in the south wall of the church at Brynderslev, in Hjørring
Shire and Børglum Hundred, whence it was long ago removed to the Round Tower. Probably it
was originally placed in the church to commemorate the consecration and dedication in the name
of CHRIST, and to perpetuate the name of the Founder or Architect. It is 4-sided, about 4 feet
8 inches long, each side 1 foot broad. Lower runes 10 inches high, the upper a little shorter.

Worm gave only the lower line of runes; perhaps the top of the stone was then hidden.
No one has yet observed the plain R between the two lines at the end of the stone. It was placed
here, as there was no room for it in the long line.

Besides the bind-rune AN in MANOM, we have also the ties UN (thrice) and AR.

We begin below from left to right, ending with the *right* half of the upper line. Then
we take the *left* half of the top line:

KIRKIA IR KRISTI KÆNT, MANOM TIL MISKUNTAR.

SUIN SUN KARMUNTAR.

This-CHURCH is CHRIST's KENNED (known, made known, named), to-MEN TILL (to, for) MISKEN
(mercy, pity).

(This is named Christ's Church, for the salvation of men.)

SUIN SON OF-KARMUNT.

We have here the Latin genitive KRISTI, instead of the Danish KRISTS. The mark K
for K in this word, also perhaps a Latinism, has its parallel on a few other stones.

BRYNDERSLEV, NORTH-JUTLAND.

.

VALTHIOFSTAD, ICELAND.

? DATE ABOUT A. D. 1100—1200.

A beautiful Door of Pinewood (drift-timber), rounded off above, 6 feet 7½ inches Danish high by 3 feet 1½ inches broad, one of the finest specimens of olden wood-carving in Europe. It was formerly in the head entrance to the ancient Church at Valþjófstað, Norðrmulasýsla, East Iceland, came to the Museum in 1851, and is elegantly drawn and chemityped by J. Magnus Petersen in Worsaae's »Nordiske Oldsager« (No. 505 in Ed. 2, No. 388 in Ed. 1).

In 1853 Prof. Sv. Grundtvig pointed out (Danmarks gamle Folkeviser, 1, p. 130) that this carving represented the Fight of King Theoderik (Diderik) with the Winged Dragon to free the perishing Lion, but the runic inscription has never yet been redd. It is more than ordinarily difficult, from injury, from the veins in the tree, and from the absence of the beginning. A slip of one plank from top to bottom has been broken off while the door was yet in Iceland, and a new piece has been put in, whereby the first few staves have been lost. At the same time the Lock was taken away and replaced with wood.

The whole surface is filled with 2 large roundels, carved in relief. Between them is a decorated Iron Ring, inlaid with silver. The lower circle shows a group of intertwined Winged Worms. The upper roundel in its lower compartment exhibits the victory of the champion over the Dragon, its 3 young ones just seen in a small den on the right, while in the upper section we have the King on horseback followed by the grateful Lion. Further to the right, beneath and outside a Church, rests the same or some other Lion on a slab bearing a small Cross and carved with runic letters 1 inch high. The noble beast is either guarding his-master while he thanks God within, or else is a symbol of the submission of heathen strength to the mild Christ. Later this may have been taken as a representation of the faitful creature dying on his master's grave.

The runic line was originally 10½ inches long, of which 9 inches remain. I take the runes to be, restoring the lost letters:

(ᛌᛁᚱ : ᛋᛁᚨ : ᛋᛁᛦ) ᚱᛁᚼᛁᛁᛦᛅᛏᛅᛁᚠ : ᛇᛁᚱ : ᛦᚱᛅᚴᛁᚠ : ᛁᚴᛖᛁᚬᚱᛁᚠ ᛒᛁᛏᛁ :

These I would divide and translate:

(HER SIA HIN) RIKIA KUNUNG HER GRAFIN ER UA DREKA ÞENA.
(Here see that) RICH (mighty) KING HERE GRAVEN (sculptured) AS (who) WONI (slew) DRAKE (dragon) THIS.

There are here 2 bindrunes, the DR and the AR in DREKA ÞENA.

It is clear enough that this carving refers to KING THEODORIK AND THE LION, but the treatment differs from the tale as told in the Vilkina Saga and yet later legends. The kemp here fights on horseback not on foot, and there is not the episode which makes him kill the young Dragons. All is here older and simpler, and the style and costume at once remind us of the Bayeux Tapestry.

BRATTAHLID, GREENLAND.

? DATE ABOUT A. D. 1200—1300.

(See C. C. Rafn, Antiquitates Americanæ, 4to. Hafniæ 1837, p. 342—4, Tab. 8, Fig. 1, Grønlands historiske Mindesmærker, Vol. 3, 8vo. Kjøbenhavn 1845, p. 812, Tab. 9, Fig. 2. Rafns Prée, p. 235; Rasks saml. Afhandl. 3, 426.)

Was found (? in 1829) at the east end of the church, in the graveyard of the old Herred-church at the Northern arm of the Igalikko fiord, east of Julianehåb, and was sent to Denmark in 1830 by J. Mathiesen, the Governor of the colony. Thus it is from Brattahlid, Eriksfiord, Greenland's Eastern settlement. It is a thin slab, broken at both ends, now about 5 feet 3 inches long and 14 inches broad, of red sandstone. The inscription runs:

ᚢᛁᚴᛑᛁᛌ : ᛘᛑ : ᚼ
ᚢᛁᛚᛁᚱ : ᚼᛂᚱ : ᚴᛚ
ᛂᛑᛂ : ᚴᚢᚦ : ᛌᛆᛚ · ᚼᛂ
ᚿᛆᚱ :

VIGDIS M. D. HVILIR HER. GLEÐE GUÞ SAL HENAR.

VIGDIS M's Daughter WHILES (rests) HERE. GLADDEN GOD SOUL HER!

M and D are contractions, M for some name beginning with M (for instance MAGNUS or MAR, &c.), and D for DOTTIR.

GRUND, ICELAND.

? DATE ABOUT A. D. 1200—1300.

(See Antiqvarisk Tidsskrift, 8vo. Kjøbenhavn 1843—45, p. 57—64. G. Stephens in Illustreret Tidende, Kjøb. den 1 Marts 1868.)

In Antiqv. Tidsskrift Fin Magnusen has given a learned and valuable description of *two ancient Icelandic Chairs*, from Grund in Oljords Syssel, Iceland's North-Amt, presented to him by Hr. Olaf Briem of Store Grund in 1843, and by himself given to the Museum. Both these Chairs are beautifully engraved in the above treatise, and the rune-covered one also in Worsaae's Nordiske Oldsager, 2nd ed. 8vo. No. 556. As far as I can see, these Chairs are of the same date, and the runes they bear seem to be as old as the »Stools« themselves.

These rich and elegant articles are of Cornel-wood, carved with a whittle, without iron nails except a few small tacks. Intended to stand against a wall, their backs are almost bare of ornament. The seats form a chest, one of which has had a lock and key. Both are variously decorated with dragon- and arabesque-work, medallions, foliage, &c.

The first has a back-piece 3 feet 4 inches high, 3 feet 11 inches broad, and 2 feet 3 inches deep. Its seat is 1 foot 2 inches high, 2 feet 5 inches broad, and 13 inches deep. It has no runes, except ℝ᛭ (ᴋ ᴇ) on its left side and some letters behind, rightly interpreted by F. Magnusen as Carpenter's-marks. They were intended to guide him in putting the pieces together, answering to *numbers*. Thus on the top of the back were formerly 9 slim sticks or round pillars, probably curiously figure-carved. Only the foot of each is left in its socket, but we can see that it has been held fast by a tiny iron cub, hammered in behind. Doubtless on these pillars, behind, were inscribed marks answering to those now on the back-piece, namely:

$$\text{�} \quad \text{J H G F E D C B A}$$

The letters are taken from right to left. Lower down, above the small loose bars which have been let in between the top and bottom pieces, are similar staves, first on the back-piece above each bar and then *repeated* on the bar itself, that there might be no mistake when they were put together. They are:

$$\text{E D C B A}$$

But the B on the bar is turned round (ꝏ).

The second Chair is somewhat less than the other. It has had no rods at the top, but on the back, carved *on* and *under* the 2 first and the 2 last of the 5 ornamented bars,

$$\text{J M T A}$$

The *lower* J-stave is reverst (ſ).

But on the front, at the very top, along the band, between the rosettes, is risted:

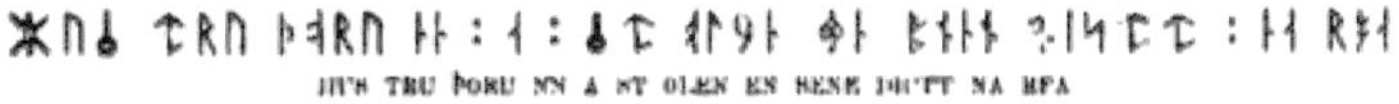

$$\text{ᛒᚾᛟ ᛏᚱᚾ ᚦᚨᚱᚾ ᚼᚼ : ᛌ : ᛌᛏ ᛌᛏᚤᚼ ᚦᛁ ᛒᚼᚼᛌ ᚵᛁᚼᛏᛏ : ᚼᚼ ᚱᚦᚼ}$$

HU'S TRU ÞORU NN A ST OLEN EN BENE DICTT NA BFA

The first part of this line, or

HUSTRU ÞORUNN A STOLEN

HOUSE-FRU (Mistress) THORUNN OWNS (possesses) STOOL-THE (this chair)

is clear enough. But the second

EN BENEDICTT NARFA

is obscure, perhaps a word or two being understood. I take it to mean:

EN (but) BENEDICT NARFSON (gave-me to-her).

On the front of the seat, above the signs of the Zodiac, we have, carved partly in runes and partly in Latin-Gothic letters:

$$\text{ᛒᚼᚦ : ᛁᚼ : ᛌᚼᚾᛌᚱᛁᛌ}$$
$$\text{ᛒᚼᚦ · ᛁᚼ · ᚴᛁᛒᛌᛁ S}$$
$$\text{ᛒᚼᚦ : ᛁᚼ : ᛌᚱᛁᛌᛏᚼ}$$

SOL IN TAURO
SOL IN GEMINE
SOL IN CANCRO
SOL IN LEONE
SOL I UIRGINE
SOL I LARBO

SOL IN AQUARIA (=Aquario).
SOL IN PISCIS (=Piscibus).
SOL IN ARIETE.

SOL I SCORPIONE
SOL I SAGITTERIO
SOL I CAPRICORNI

Below the same signs are the Months:

ᛁᚼᚠᚿᛁᚱᛁᚿᛒ   ᚠᛁᛒᚱᚿᛁᚱᛁᚿᛒ   �ᚼᛁᚿᛒ
ᛁᚠᚱᛁᚠᛋ   �478ᛁᚿᛋ   ᛁᚿᛁᛁᚿᛋ
ᛁᚿᚠᛁᚿᛒ   ᛁᚿᚥᚿᛒᛏᚿᛋ   ᛒᛁᚲᛏᛁᛦᛒᛁᛐ
ᛁᚼᛏᛁᛒᛁᛐ   ᛁᛁᚿᛁᛦᛒᛁᛐ   ᛉᛁᚼᛁᛦᛒᛐ

Thus the ABC of this artist has been:

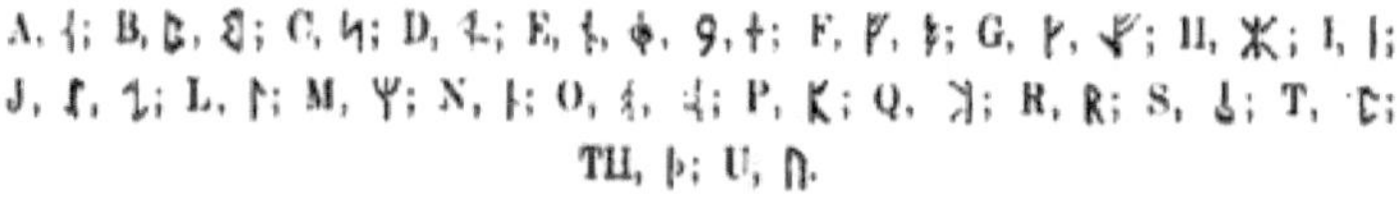

A, ᛁ; B, ᛒ, ᛏ; C, ᚼ; D, ᛐ; E, ᛁ, ᚦ, ᚼ, ᛏ; F, ᚠ, ᚦ; G, ᛝ, ᚥ; H, ᛞ; I, ᛁ;
J, ᛁ, ᛎ; L, ᛁ; M, ᛦ; N, ᛁ; O, ᚦ, ᚼ; P, ᚴ; Q, ᛉ; R, R; S, ᛁ; T, ᛐ;
TH, þ; U, ᚾ.

The runes on the front of the Runic Chair average nearly half an inch in height.

Fin Magnusen thinks that these chairs originally belonged to Holum Cathedral or to Medrevalle Monastery, and that they commemorated JON OGMUNDSSON, the Patron Saint of Holum See. In this case, the line beginning HUSTRU HOMUNS must have been added at the Reformation.

Since the above was written, another runic discovery has been made with regard to this chair. I had remarkt that both the stools were attackt by the worm, which were making great ravages. State-councilor Worsaae at once directed Mr. Steffensen, the Conservator, to boil them in Petroleum &c. for their preservation. That gentleman commenced with the rune-bearer in September 1867, and took it to pieces for further treatment. In so doing he found one of the pieces of the back, which *outside* is merely decorated with a deeply carved

covered on the *inside* (now first visible) with a number of runes. Archivary Herbst kindly drew my attention to this remarkable find, and on examination I deciphered the runes as a rudely and carelessly cut RUNIC ALPHABET in the order of the Latin ABC. I here give this interesting piece of wood, drawn and chemityped *full size* by J. Magnus Petersen.

We have here evidently 3 lines of runes. The first contains 10 letters, the staves A to K; the second 14, the staves L to Z; the third 4, the staves A to D, in a modified alphabet. As usual on such pieces, we are somewhat hampered by accidental dints and scratches and pieces which have scaled off, and by the grain of the wood; but I believe that I am correct in reading the characters as follows, giving to them their normal shape:

A B C D E F G   H I K

L M N O P   Q R S T U X Y Z

The following | seems to be a closing mark. Then come apparently:

A B C D

On the edge below, part of which is shaved away, are also traces of letters, tho they have been cut thro in the middle by the deep groove. We can still see spores of what may have been an ◊ (o), and then the tops and bottoms of

P P Q Q

Thus the q is here a variation of the one given above.

I think that, when the chair was making, one of the boys or men amused himself in an idle hour with roughly carving the runic alphabet with his knife on this piece, which was afterwards used for a part of the work. And this is another proof of the commonness of the runes — whose alphabets are so very numerous — and of their not being at this early period merely «secret and magical characters».

PIEDSTED, NORTH JUTLAND.

? DATE ABOUT A. D. 1200–1300.

Oaken lid of the ark or strong box of Piedsted Church, in Veile Shire, Diocese of Ribe. This ancient Church-chest was destroyed early in this century, but State-Councilor Worsaae happily rescued the lid in 1840 and transported it to the capital. It is about 4 feet 5 inches long by 18 inches wide, and nearly 2 inches thick. The top has been richly decorated with wrought iron-work in the olden style, — now all torn away, tho much of the pattern can yet be made out.

On the inside the maker has named himself in boldly cut runes, as follows:

ᚴᚢᚾᛁ · ᛋᛘᛁᚦ : ᚠᛅᚦ : ᛘᛁᚴ

KUNNI SMIÞ GARÞ MÆK
KUNNI, SMITH, GAR'D (made) ME.

The top of the first 2 runes is injured, but there is no sign of any dot in the ᚠ, which was therefore K, not G. So we have MÆK, not MÆG. Yet we have GARÞ, not KARÞ. But such variations in form (antique) monuments are familiar and common.

The dot in the 3rd rune is apparently clear, and as old as the rest of the carving. In this case it doubles the letter, and the word is thus KUNNI, not KUNI.

As we see, the inscription is in good Jutlandish.

SØRUP, FYN.

? DATE ABOUT A. D. 1200–1300.

(See Antiqvariske Annaler, Vol. 3, Kjøbenhavn 1820, p 353)

Found in 1816 by Pastor Bredsdorff in Sørup Church; given to the Museum by Baroness Rantzau-Lehn of Hvidkilde. Greatest height about 6 feet 8 inches, greatest breadth about 2 feet 4, letters from 3 to 4 inches long. At the top of the stone is carved what looks to be a large Lion, and thereunder a Greek Cross. On each side is a runic band, close to the edge. In this, on the left, are carved:

ᚼᛁ : ᚱᚦᚠᛁ : ᛁᛁᚢᛋᛁᛏᚼᛁ · ᛂᛁ

On the right, beginning below:

ᚠᚦ · ᚼᚱᛂᛁᚼ·ᛁᚼᛁ · ᚢᚱᛂᚠᛒ (ᛁ or ᚦ or ᚱ)

On the right edge, from above downwards:

ᛁᚼᛁᚠᚢᚦᚱ · ᛏᛂᚠ · ᛁᚼᛁᛅᛏ · ᛂᛁ

Some of the letters are worn and indistinct, or injured by the scaling off of the surface. What the whole meant I cannot say. Probably we have here an inscription *so strongly contracted* that we shall never be able to read it.

ÚTSKÁLAR, ICELAND.

? DATE ABOUT A. D. 1200—1300.

(See Antiqvarisk Tidsskrift, 1843—5, p 102, 188.)

Came to the Museum in 1844 from the graveyard at Útskálar, Gullbringusýsla, S. W. Iceland. Only a fragment of dark stone, greatest height about 17¼ inches, greatest breadth about 15, and about 3 to 4 inches thick. Runes on right side, if any, gone; on left side very faint. I take them to be:

... (R)BIR · (PIRÞⴖ · ΥI) ...

which may perhaps have been:

... (R)HER (GERÞU ME)rki ...
N. N. and ARBER GARED this-MARK after .....

ÚTSKÁLAR, ICELAND.

? DATE ABOUT A. D. 1300--1400.

(See Antiqvarisk Tidsskrift 1843—45, Kjøbenhavn 1845, p. 102, 188.)

Came to the Museum in 1844 from the graveyard at Útskálar Church, Gullbringusýsla, S. W. Iceland. Greatest height about 2 feet 9 inches, greatest breadth about 14 inches, greatest thickness about 7 inches. Average length of the runes about 2½ inches. The inscription runs in 3 perpendicular lines, and is now first deciphered. But the surface never was drest, and in addition hereto the stone has suffered many injuries. Many of the letters are barely legible. Those which are unusually doubtful I have placed between ( ). A piece of the stone has been broken off below, and one stave (R) has there been lost. Otherwise the whole is seemingly complete. I take the whole risting to have been, (beginning with the center line, then that on the left, then that on the right):

ᚻᛁᚦᚱ ᛬ ᚻᚾᛁᚠᚦᚱ ᛬ ᛒᚱᚦᛏᛁ(ᛗᛏ) ᛬ ᛏᚱᚤᛦ
ᚠᛏᛁᛁᚦᚱ ᛬ ᛏᚦᛦᚦᛒ ᛬ (ᚦᚱ) ᛬ ᚲᛏᛁᚦᚱ ᛬ ᚻᛦᛒᛏᚦ
ᚱᛁᚠᛂ ᛬ ᚱᚦᚱ ᛬ ᛦᛏᛏ ᛬ (ᚱ)ᚦᛏ ᛬ (ᛦ)ᚦᚱ

HER HULER BRETI(UA) ORMS DOTTER

LESEÞ (ER) PATER NOSTE(R)

RIFZ RER;

SAL (R)EN (S)ER.

HERE WHILES (rests, slumbers) BRETHA ORMS-DAUGHTER.

LEESE (read, say, pray, bede) YE a-PATER NOSTER-for-her-soul.

RIVES-is the KA (body),

the-SOUL RUNS (hastens, wings her way) for-HERSELF.

These two lines in English stave-rime:

FAIL, FLESH! — FROM THEE

THE SOUL SPEEDS FREE!

For this happy translation of the difficult SAL REN SER I am indebted to Prof. Gislason. This is the thought so elegantly exprest by a modern Scandinavian (Esaias Tegnér):

Lätt skall lösta anden hitta	Light the loosen'd Soul then glideth
Vägen ifrån jordens bryn.	Far away from this poor earth.

The later rune ⟂ is very rarely used. It is sometimes carved for Y, sometimes for Z. Here, as we see, it is plainly Z.

<hr>

GUFUDAL, ICELAND.

? DATE ABOUT A. D. 1400—1500.

[See Antiqvarisk Tidsskrift 1843–45, 8vo   Kjøbenhavn 1845. p. 109, 183.]

This sill (Pillar) of Basalt was sent to the Museum from Iceland in 1844, but is now first accessible to the public. It was obtained by Althingsman Jon Sigurdsson from Pastor Olaf Sivertsen of Flatey, and came from the graveyard of Gufudal Church, in Barðastrandarsýsla, North-west of Iceland. Its runes have not yet been redd. It is tall and 5-sided, about 4 feet high, each face about 5 inches broad. The runes are nearly 4 inches long. Near the top are 5 shallow holes, in the shape of an equal-limbed Cross. Lines run down each of the faces, but runes are carved within them only on the left side. These begin at the bottom and run upwards. The last letter is 15 inches from the top of the stone. The first Cross-hole is 12 inches from the top. All the staves are tolerably clear, and read:

᛬ ᚻᛦᚱ ᛬ ᛚᛁᚠᚾᚱ ᛬ ᛒᚱᛦᚱ ᛬ ᛁᚾᛦᚱ ᛬ ᛁᚠ ᛬ ᛁᛏᛒ

HER LIGUR PRER; IUAN, 10, ION.

HERE LIE THREE-persons: IUAN, 10 and ION.

Very striking is the plain use here of LIGUR, the 3rd person *singular*, instead of LIGIA, the 3rd person *plural*; thus showing an early instance, in Iceland itself, of that use of singular verbs for plural which has gained so strong a footing in the Danish dialect. And yet we have to, well known in compounds, but here found for the first time in Scandinavia as an uncompounded name. Observe also the ÞRER for ÞRIR, as in Old-Swedish.

The formula here is very uncommon. But there is a parallel on the Ugglum stone, near Falkeping, West Gotland, Sweden, (flitted i 1863 to the Stockholm Museum). This is No. 939 in Bautil, No. 1642 in Liljegren, and is a coped or coffin stone elegantly carved in relief. It is 6 feet 6 inches Swedish long by 21 Swedish inches broad. I possess a very fine drawing made by Intendant G. Brusewitz in 1860. From this large and correct copy I give the runes:

✝ ᚦᚱᛁᚱ · ᛚᛁᚵᚵᛁᛅ · ᛘᛅᚿᚿ · ᚢᚿᛏᛁᚱ · ᚦᛅᛘᛘᛅ · ✝
✝ ᛋᛏᛁᚿᛁ : ᚵᚢᚿᚿᛅᚱᚱ : ᛋᛁᚼᚢᛅᛏᚱ · ᚼᛅᛚᛋᛏᛁᚿᚿ ✝

ÞRIR LIGGIA MÆNN UNDIR ÞÆMMÆ
STENE; GUNNARR, SHIVATR, HALSTENN.
THREE LIE MEN (three men lie) UNDER THIS STONE; GUNNAR, SHIVAT and HALSTEN.

As we had on the Icelandic pillar the »neology« LIGUR, so we have here the »archaisms« ÞÆMMÆ STENE (dat. s. m.), RR in GUNNARR, &c.

HVALSNES, ICELAND.

? DATE ABOUT A. D. 1400—1500.

(See Antiqvarisk Tidsskrift, 1843—5, 8vo, Kjøbenhavn 1845, p. 102, 133.)

Came to the Museum in 1844 from the graveyard of Hvalsnes Church, south-west Iceland, Gullbringusýsla. It is a small graystone block, greatest height about 1 foot 9 inches, average breadth about 1 foot, average thickness about 6 inches. Runes about 2½ inches high. The lower part of the stone is gone. The risting shows a simple Cross, each limb composed of two broad bands; between these, in the center or stem, from above downwards, run the runes. As the stone has never been drest the letters are rough, and here and there have suffered. The last stave but one was ᚵ (G); next came ᚱ, but of this only part remains. This of course was followed by ETA, and perhaps by a word or two of prayer for the dead. What is now left is:

ᚼᛂᚱᚼᚢᛁᛚᛁᚱᛘᛆᚱᚵ(ᚱ)...

HER HUILIR MARG(reta).
HERE WHILES (rests, lies, reposes) MARGRETA (Margaret).